GARDENING the
UNCOMMITTED

What you really need to know
when you don't really want to know

by Catherine McMillan

© 2020 Catherine McMillan

ISBN: 9798639295034

www.uncommittedgardener.co.uk

Introduction

Does your gardening experience consist of buying random plants from the garden centre, taking them home and watching them slowly die?

Do you suspect the alternative involves spending every spare moment in the shed like a 1950s husband trying to avoid ''er indoors', carrying out dubious-sounding practices such as 'chitting' and 'pricking out'? Even when it's cold. And raining.

It doesn't have to. This book tells you what you really need to know. Which definitely doesn't include chitting.

Don't learn it all

There are many rules to gardening, and there are also exceptions to all these rules.

Which does, unfortunately, make things potentially tricky. Sorry.

But you can still have a garden that is half-decent rather than half-dead - without devoting your life to it - by learning a few of the rules that really matter.

You don't need to grow from seeds, you don't need to learn the difference between John Innes no 1 and John Innes no 2, and you don't need to know what you are supposed to do with those things in the garden centre that look like upside-down salad crispers.

Gardening is a vast, vast topic. Huge. That is why proper gardening books are so big.

According to Google there are around 400,000 different species of plant. And that is why you think you don't know much. You don't, and you never will. Even Monty Don doesn't know that many plants.

Fortunately, a great number of these won't grow willingly in your garden and a great many more will hold no appeal to you.

Sorry, we don't feel you're right for this garden

From the remainder find some favourites and don't ever worry about what you don't know.

It's the taking part ...

As such a wide-open subject you will find there are numerous opinions on how to do just about everything, often completely contradictory.

There is only one sensible way to approach this: do whatever fits closest to what you can be bothered to do, when you can be bothered to do it.

If your Uncle Ken says to cut your lavender bushes in spring, and your friend Sara says to cut them in autumn, assume either way will work well enough.

Maybe one method gives better results than the other, but we are not aiming for a Chelsea Gold Medal here; if the plant doesn't die and it still flowers next year then job done.

Whatever you do, you are going to have to expend at least some effort. Low maintenance is not the same as no maintenance. There is no such thing as no maintenance. I repeat: No Such Thing.

Your living room requires regular vacuuming, dusting, tidying and cushion-plumping - and occasional decorative overhauls - to keep it looking reasonable and you should expect to have to put in the same amount of work in the garden.

Trial and error

There are several phases to your gardening life.

Initially you will buy plants because they are beautiful, amazing, wow, look at the flowers on that. You don't know what you are doing, they are probably not suited to your conditions, and they die.

You then find yourself increasingly fond of anything that survives, full of admiration and wonder at The Plant That Doesn't Die. You'll probably buy several more of them.

In time you might gain enough experience to get the hang of this gardening malarkey and venture back to the headturners.

The Lingo

There are so many technical terms in gardening that it can feel like a foreign language (It usually is: Latin). But there is no need to get a degree in Classics before you get started.

'Perennial' means the plant will come back year after year (think of the phrase "perennial favourite"). In the winter it will probably give a good impersonation of being dead. It probably won't be.

'Annuals' live just one year.

'Deciduous' means all the leaves fall off in winter. 'Evergreen' means they don't.

'Foliage' is the fancy word for leaves.

'Hardy' means it will not shrivel up and die at the first sign of frost.
'Tender' means it probably will.

Don't worry too much about the rest.

The practicalities

Don't bite off more than you can chew

With time, money, skill and a degree of compromise, you can achieve almost anything.

But you don't have these in unlimited supply, otherwise you wouldn't be reading this book.

Yes, you can have a tropical garden in East Anglia, but not if you are only planning on spending an afternoon a month working in the garden, and don't want to spend the entirety of September wrapping it all up in fleece. And have a budget in the very low hundreds.

.

Go with the flow(er)

What conditions can you offer the potential residents of your garden?

Sometimes plants will die because you are rubbish, sometimes because they are rubbish and sometimes it was never going to work, however much willing there was on either side.

Roses will starve in sandy soils, succulents will rot in clay soils, gold-leaved shrubs will wither in scorching sun, herbs will be pitiful in the shade.

So, actually, it's really quite simple:

Work out what the conditions are in your garden and then buy plants that like those conditions.

Failsafe (no refunds).

How to choose a plant, part 1:

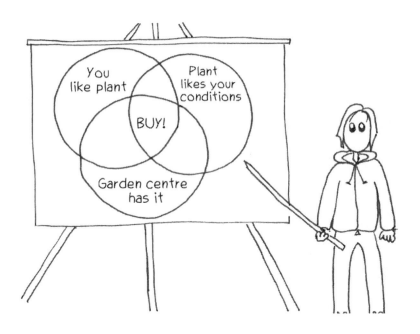

Curtain twitching

If it grows well in your neighbours' gardens, chances are it will grow well for you. Just don't copy that retired couple who spend every daylight hour working in the garden – they are operating at expert level.

If you don't know the names of any plants, take photos with you to the nursery or garden centre, where staff should be able to help.

If you never see a favourite plant of yours in the neighbourhood, take this as a heavy hint that it probably doesn't grow well in the local climate or soils (or that you are living amongst luddites who wouldn't know a magnificent plant if it slapped them round the face).

There is a reason why the farm shop never has locally grown lemons.

How to choose a plant, part 2:

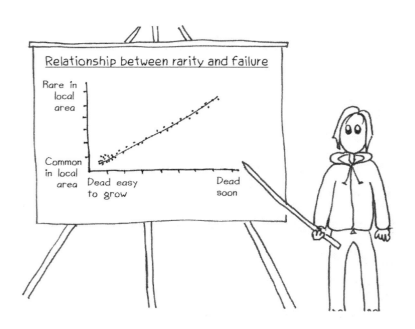

Freezing their buds off

Considering temperature will immediately allow you to strike off huge swathes of plants.

Most parts of Britain can go as low as -15c. Meanwhile, those fabulous Bougainvilleas you saw everywhere on your Mediterranean holiday will die if nighttime temperatures go much below +10c (which they will).

Conclusion: Bougainvilleas are not a good choice for the uncommitted British gardener.

If your local garden centre has it displayed inside assume it probably won't survive winter.

City gardens, walled gardens and southern coastal gardens are usually warmer than elsewhere, but you will still be pushing your luck with anything that cannot cope with lower than -5c.

Seeing the light

Now, aspect – where is your garden in relation to your house?

If it is south of the house then the estate agent would have been sure to mention this; the house will shelter the garden from cold northerly winds whilst blocking out very little sunlight.

West is next sunniest, then east, then north, which will be coolest and shadiest of all (probably).

If your plot is hemmed in by buildings on all sides, this is all largely irrelevant. Carry on your way.

Most parts of your garden will be in shade for at least some of the day.

More than six hours in the middle of the day is considered full sun, less than two hours is deep shade.

There are many lovely spring-flowering plants that will grow in a woodland setting but that is because the trees have yet to regrow their leaves, so it isn't actually very shady.

If your light is being blocked by a brick wall, those bluebells aren't going to be so enthusiastic.

Please (please, seriously) accept that flowers don't like deep shade - embrace the chance to create a peaceful, understated, leafy area (or get in a tree surgeon/demolition operative to address the source of the problem).

Soil's boring; soil matters

Now look at the soil.

No, do not turn the page, this is vitally important.

If puddles form on it, it is poorly drained; if it is reminiscent of muddy sand, it is sandy; if there are lots of stones in it, it is stony; if there is lots of chalk in it, it is chalky; if you could mould it into vases, it is clay; if you cannot think of any way of describing it other than "brown", congratulations: you probably have average soil and can grow pretty much anything.

If it already looks like the contents of a bag of multipurpose compost you have hit horticultural jackpot. Gloat. After all, how often in life do you get the chance to?

Most plants don't care too much about soil acidity, so you needn't either.

Suffice to say, soil acidity is usually tied in with the hardness of your water, for geological reasons that are of no more interest to you now than they were during that school geography lesson you didn't pay attention to.

As a rule of thumb, if you spend an ungodly amount of time scouring limescale from your kitchen and bathroom, you probably have alkaline soil and shouldn't bother with the likes of Rhododendrons, Azaleas and Pieris, which thrive on iron-rich acidic soils and sulk and starve on limey alkaline soils.

400,000 plants whittled right down

With these bits of basic observation complete you can now look up lists of plants that will thrive in your conditions.

This will probably involve some cross-referencing to match your garden - what turns up in clay soil lists AND windy site lists?

You can push your luck so far, according to the ratio of your arm length/pocket depth, but if your borders are boggy and shady do not waste your money on something that likes sandy and sunny.

The
creative bit

Design

So, you have found yourself in possession of a garden. Your garden, to do with as you please.

Even if it is rented – in fact you should consider this the perfect opportunity to discover that some rather attractive, commercially available plants are massively invasive. You do not want to find this out once you have put them in the garden of your 'Forever home'.

Please yourself

You have got your lists of what should thrive on your plot, your lists of what might and now you can find out what pleases you. Peer into other people's plots, flick through magazines and click through websites.

Is it the geometric beds that make your heart sing, the symmetrical ones, the wild rambling gardens, the oh-so-sophisticated white borders, leafy flower-free areas, or hot, fiery, clashing blooms?

If spelling out your name in hot-pink primroses will amuse you, then do it: It's your garden.

Planting like a pro

The average suburban garden has a lawn in the centre surrounded by stingy borders containing single plants rowed up along the fence like they are waiting for the firing squad.

William Wordsworth was moved to poetry by the sight of *a crowd, a host* of golden daffodils. Not a single daffodil, a tulip, a 'I'm not sure of the proper name but I call it elephant's ears', one of those things you see in car parks and a 'I don't know what it is; it was here when we moved in but it's quite attractive in the summertime'.

It is a beginner's mistake to buy one of everything: if you buy 50 different plants, you then need to remember how to care for 50 different plants.

Find ten plants you like and then buy five of each*. Because there is only so much space in your brain for this sort of stuff.

Make your borders deep enough that you can plant in clumps - in odd numbers for a natural look, even numbers for symmetry - and repeat through the garden for a cohesive look. This is what happens in nature, and is what a fancy garden designer would do for you in exchange for a large sack of cash.

Trees and large shrubs don't need to be clumped, but two or three of the same variety dotted about can have the same pleasing effect.

*You'll need to buy way more than 50 plants, but let's not think about that now.

If this all sounds too joylessly tasteful you can still keep things simple by buying different varieties of the same plant.

For example, get three blue Lupins, three in yellow, three in red and three in pink. You will get a riot of colour but they will all want the same care: they will flower at the same time, want cutting down at the same time and will get those massive aphids Lupins are prone to at the same time, which is all much easier to keep track of.

Among those ten different plants you should be looking for a good mix of shapes - in terms of flowers and leaves as well as the plants in their entirety - as well as sizes.

Too many flumpy plants looks Eeyore-ish, too many towering spires is all exclamation mark and no substance.

Have a bit of up and down too. You will be able to see most borders from the side, and above from bedroom windows, so you do not have to slavishly put shortest plants at the front and tallest at the back.

Gardening style

If your garden fantasy involves you wafting around with a pair of secateurs in a floppy hat and floaty dress (and who am I to judge how a man spends his free time. Boom boom. Sigh) then you will want plants that like "regular deadheading".

This means you go out every few days to snip off the old flowers to just above a new bud or flower to encourage new blooms. Contenders include Dahlias, Roses, Sweet Peas and Cosmos.

If you are a hacker, almost anything that doesn't have woody growth can get chopped to the ground in early spring, late autumn or when it finishes flowering (author not responsible for death of any plants that are exception to this rule - see page 2).

Buddleias, Dogwoods, Willows, Smoke Bushes, Hebes, Elderberries and Fuchsias are among the shrubs that will (usually) shrug off a winter/spring butchering (no refunds), as will most perennials.

If your household includes boisterous dogs, children or partners, do not buy anything brittle looking. Get hacker-friendly plants that can cope with having branches snapped off, and flumpy plants, which will usually spring back.

If you wish to discourage the aforementioned destructive garden users, get thorny and/or spiky plants (and a decent pair of gauntlet gloves).

If even an annual chop sounds too much, there are some evergreen plants that theoretically need no regular attention from you, such as Pittosporums, Phormiums, Rhododendrons, Camellias, ornamental grasses and ferns, but nothing is straightforward in this life, and they won't grow in every situation.

Parting with your cash

Tools

If you are buying a tool that is supposed to be sharp, spend enough money so that it is actually sharp. Scissors that uselessly mash stems are annoying.

If you are buying a hose, don't buy a narrow one. You will only get a pitiful dribble out of it and it will take ages to water your plants. Which will be annoying.

If you have sticky clay soil, buy stainless steel forks and spades. The soil will stick to any other sort of metal. Which will be annoying.

If you have thorny plants, buy some decent thornproof gloves. They are amazing. Do not attempt to do anything else in them. You have greater dexterity in oven gloves.

Do not buy anything else until a frustrating hour in the garden has led you to the conclusion that it is the solution to all your troubles.

The time to buy a trowel is when you wish your spade was much, much smaller, loppers when you really wish your secateurs could reach another foot or two, kneepads when you cannot walk properly anymore and a twine dispenser when ... I don't know, I have yet to stumble across that scenario.

Similarly, do not rush into getting a greenhouse until you have thoroughly antagonised every other member of the household by covering all windowsills and sunlight-dappled surfaces with your seedling collection.

Because unless you have become smitten with the process of propagation it will become nothing more than an eminently breakable see-through shed in which you keep your knee pads and twine dispenser.

I think we should buy a lawnmower

Find a good seller

The number of people who will stride into a nursery and proclaim they know nothing about plants is, frankly, astonishing. If you have made the mistake of entering a less than honourable establishment you might as well be shouting: "I will believe anything you tell me: please rinse me of all my cash."

Definitely take any opportunity to tap staff for useful advice and plant suggestions but make it clear you are worth cultivating as a customer. Tell them you will buy a handful of recommended plants today, and if they do well, will be back for more.

This should greatly improve your chances of being sent away with the most appropriate plants in the healthiest condition.

Not all purveyors of plants are created equal.

A plant might turn up its heels not because of your ineptitude but because of what happened in its early nursery life.

Pile 'em high and flog 'em cheap plants have often been grown with artificial heat and light to encourage quick growth. These battery-farmed specimens are often weak and underfed and prone to collapse when introduced to the real world.

We must not make generalisations, but consider buying your plants from outlets whose original business plan wasn't based on the sale of baked beans and breakfast cereals, nor screw sets and shelving.

Somewhere that specialises in them, perhaps.

Avoiding duds

In the main, bushiest is bestest. If there is only one measly stem poking out of the pot, and it dies or breaks, that is it, game over. Ten stems and one dies, who cares?

Unless the label says it is supposed to have gold leaves, the plant with the deepest green colouring will probably be the healthiest and therefore most likely to succeed.

A plant limply flopping about like a sulky teenager is not a good sign, unless it is labelled as trailing or carpeting.

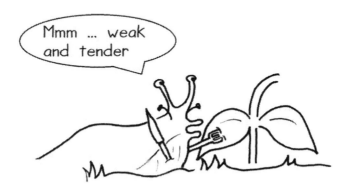

Plant prices

Cost does not necessarily equal quality. If a plant seems expensive compared with the other plants at the same garden centre it is probably because it is either slow to grow or difficult to grow.

If it is the latter, you might as well save yourself the time and hassle and just throw your money directly onto the compost heap you do not have because you are not that keen on gardening.

(At the other end of the scale, beware friends bearing free plants. It may be a great act of charity, but many's the gardener who has offloaded clumps of the massively invasive perennial they have just weeded out on to unsuspecting saps. Narrow your eyes and consider how good a friend they really are before accepting.)

Plant through the seasons

If you are planting up a new border and you want it to look interesting all year round, you will either need good plant knowledge and strong powers of imagination … or to go to your local nursery or garden centre every few months throughout the year to buy what is looking good then.

Being honest with ourselves, you are not going to buy any plants in winter, so make sure your first shopping trip includes hardy evergreens (see page 7).

What's in a name?

The average plant label will tell you the name of the plant; the size it will grow to (be suspicious of anything saying "ten foot in five years"; this is usually a sly way of avoiding telling you that in 15 years it will be 50 foot tall); that the plant will be "best in full sun and well-drained soil" (it will say this even if it is a pond plant, so take this information with a pinch of salt); a fulsome description of the flowers and foliage, which seems unnecessary what with the label being attached to said plant where these things are abundantly apparent.

What it will rarely tell you is how to prune the plant. And this is why you need to keep the label. Because you will not remember its name. The internet can tell you how to look after your plant, but it cannot necessarily tell you what it actually is.

The label need not stay with the plant: unless you have what could legitimately be described as "grounds" you should be able to keep your labels in a box and identify the plant by process of elimination.

Size matters

You probably think you want fast-growing plants. You do not. These plants are cracking on with it because they intend to get an awful lot of growing done.

If the label says it grows to five metres and you have room for only one metre, you might well be able to keep it pruned to size, but it is likely to turn into a battle of wills as you spend yet another Sunday afternoon hacking the ruddy thing back.

Pick a plant that fits for a happy and harmonious future.

Planting ... finally!

Dig in

Digging out a new flower bed is a great way to get started: if there is nothing there, then there will be nothing you don't recognise.

If it is grassy ground, use a sharp spade to cut the fated lawn in squares, and then lever out in thin slices. You do not want to dig out too much soil, because you now have to get rid of it: the council will probably charge you to dump it at the tip, and there are unlikely to be many takers for your mossy, buttercup-choked surplus turves. (If you pile them upside-down somewhere the grass in them will eventually die, leaving you with just the soil, moss and buttercups to disperse across the garden.)

It is then worth poking about with a fork to loosen the soil a bit and to check that there isn't anything troublesome lurking under the soil that will stop your plants getting their roots down.

This is the archaeological dig stage, when you will mostly discover that your forebears liked breaking blue and white china and burying it in the garden (in my extensive experience).

If you hit something hard and large, pause a moment to consider if it could be any of the following: water pipe, gas pipe, vital root belonging to that tree just there, unexploded World War Two bomb, final resting place of beloved family pet.

If so, you might wish to think of a different location for your flower bed. Otherwise proceed gingerly.

Still banging on about soil

The single greatest thing you can do towards gardening success is to improve the soil.

Back in the 20th century, gardeners like to do something called 'double-digging' which involved digging deep trenches in the borders in order to rearrange the soil.

Because ... I don't know, they liked having bad backs?

Unless there is a hot new chiropractor in town that you would like to get acquainted with, you might prefer to use the 'no-dig' method to improve the condition of your soil: plonk some manure on top and let the worms do the rest. But, it is up to you.

Well-rotted manure (if it still looks like poo and smells like poo, it's not ready, so you can keep your jokes to yourself), compost, leaf mulch, soil conditioner, dumped on top, lightly forked in or double-dug in: all make your borders a better place for plants to grow.

The better the soil, the stronger and healthier your plants will be, the more flowers you will get and the fewer problems you will have with drainage, pests and diseases.

Potions and powders such as bonemeal or mycorrhizal fungi in the planting hole will help things along but these are the mere sugar sprinkles to the cake of organic matter like compost and manure.

Planting plants

The best time to plant plants is when they are dormant. Dozing in winter they will barely even notice they have been moved, their roots settling in without fuss or bother, what with their having nothing else on their plates.

Of course that is not when you are going to do your plant shopping. Because you have a heart and a soul. You are going to buy them when they look pretty.

This, unfortunately, is much harder for the plants because their roots are very busy finding enough food and water for the buds and flowers and foliage and they really could do without the hassle of having to settle themselves into new surroundings.

The sensible thing (having unsensibly bought the plant in full bloom), is to cut the flowers off and stick them in a vase, so the plant only has leaves and stems to deal with. Leave them on and you have made your watering responsibility that much more crucial.

"Water well until established"

For the average shrub or perennial, probably priced £5-£15, you should be pouring in the region of 3-5 litres of water around the base as soon as you plant it.

Give it another two or three good waterings in its first week, unless it rains (and this has to be proper soak-you-to-your-underpants rainfall), and probably twice more in its second week.

In my opinion, if it is not settled in by then it is not worth the bother.

Exceptions are:
1. You have been foolish enough to plant in the middle of a heatwave
2. You have really free-draining soil
3. Plants that are already sizeable, such as trees or large shrubs.

For the first two you will probably have to water daily for several weeks; for the latter you should use more water and may have to water weekly for the best part of a year.

Growing new shoots and leaves is a sign that the plant has made itself at home (aka established).

Losing leaves, on the other hand, is a bad sign.

Do not jump to the conclusion that more water is the solution. As many plants have died from too much water as not enough.

Using a trowel or something similar, see how far down you have to prod before you find wet soil. If only the top few inches are dry you should leave the watering for another day or you risk rotting the roots.

If the ground is so dry you cannot even get the trowel in, you really need to step up your watering regime.

Types of plant

Practice plants

Seasonal bedding plants, also known as patio plants, are a great way to get started. They are small and manageable and you are not expected to keep them alive for more than six months.

Think of them like the starter pets your parents made you have before they would let you have a dog. But with more scope for trying out colour combinations.

They are particularly good in pots and baskets but can also work in the borders.

Summer bedding plants can be on sale as early as March. Do not buy them then: they will die from cold. These are aimed at people with greenhouses, coldframes, propagators, fleece and bubblewrap and the horticultural dedication to go through all that hassle for the sake of saving 50p per plant. Wait till at least May before you get yours.

Springing back

Flowering bulbs are so easy you will forget what you have got, making for fresh delight every year when they pop back up.

Most nurseries and garden centres now sell potted bulbs in spring, so you can see exactly what you are getting and where they will be most effective.

To settle that particular marital dispute, you are supposed to snap the flower stems off daffodils when they finish, but let the leaves die down. However, they will almost certainly re-flower next year whatever you do.

If you never have any success with Tulips or Crocus it is probably because mice are eating the bulbs, and you should probably rethink your relationship with next door's cat.

Pretty flowers are easier than tasty veg

Many people are first drawn to the garden by the desire to grow their own, but the pitfalls are many.

Nature, raw in claw and beak and slime (and unceasing rain, late frosts and limited sunshine), will conspire against you and it is easy to become disheartened.

Earn your green fingers with ornamental plants and easy-to-grow perennial herbs – save learning about blight and sawfly and nematodes till at least year two of your gardening life.

If you must, start with salads. They are quick to grow, which has two benefits: one, there is little time for anything to go wrong; two, if it does, you will have spent so little time and effort on them you won't really care.

Wildflower borders

Wildflower borders fall into the category of things that sound like they should be easy, but aren't.

Scattering a packet of Mixed Wildflower seeds is a deeply regrettable – and all too common – error.

A wildflower is just a weed with good PR. You don't know what was actually supposed to come up so you leave it all. The pretty stuff is barely there, and all you are left with is disappointment and regret and the rubbish stuff which proliferates across the rest of the garden for ever after.

Go to the local nursery in early summer and buy up annual Cornflowers, Cosmos, Sweet Peas, Nasturtiums and Marigolds to sate your desire for somewhere to frolic through on one of the 12 days of summer when the sun properly shines.

Planting for wildlife

You do not need a wild looking garden to help the wildlife.

There are extensive lists on the internet cataloguing the very many plants that will benefit pollinating insects. If you are at a garden centre and do not have a list to hand, a friend with hayfever will serve just as well: the moment they start wheezing and their eyes puff up and redden you will know you are on to a winner.

If you are the one with hayfever, surround your seating area with lovely sterile flowers and leafy plants and banish the pollen-bathed plants to a less popular part of the garden. Nobody likes a martyr.

Problems

Weeds

A weed is a wild plant growing where it is not wanted.

The average weed is like water: it will spread to fill whatever space there is to fill.

So do not leave any space. Stick in another plant, or if that is not feasible or advisable, bark chippings will stop anything new seeding itself.

Be aware that every blackbird in the locality will make it their life's work to systematically flick every last bark chip on to the lawn on the supposition there is something to eat underneath.

You will have to decide for yourself whether replacing the bark chips is more annoying than pulling up weeds.

It will also make it more difficult for you to add manure to your borders. Which you are definitely going to do (*narrows eyes*).

When weeding, you need to pull up the root as well. Snapping off the heads will buy you some time as it will stop the inevitable explosion of seed, but only bother with this if you really do not have the time (or enthusiasm) to fetch a trowel.

Some weeds, such as bindweed, will regenerate from the teensiest fragment of root, and even the most assiduous sweeps - sweeps that even a gold panner would consider overly meticulous - will not get it all.

Others, such as dandelions, have tap roots that reach somewhere below the Earth's Asthenosphere layer.

If you have an established infestation of these you either need to accept them as a part of your life or: Get some weed spray.

Yes, you had romantic notions of gardening organically but unless you live in a solar-panelled yurt and travel everywhere by horse and cart you have far greater sins to atone for.

Pests

If you want to gain practical experience of pests and diseases, get a Rose. They attract pretty much everything.

Most pests and diseases are to be found lurking on the undersides of leaves. If it is moving it is a pest, if it is not it is a disease.

The most desirable way to deal with pests is to wait for a bigger creature to solve the problem for you, whilst you stand by humming the Circle of Life.

Ladybirds eat aphids, beetles eat small slugs, hedgehogs eat large slugs, cats eat rabbits (you probably won't find rabbits on the undersides of leaves) and so on.

If this tactic doesn't work it is time for the garden's apex predator: you.

Do not force the bloodlust. If you don't mind a few munched-up leaves, then let the beasties be. Shoot first, ask questions later is not acceptable in our ecologically-minded times.

Sometimes, however, your outrage at the damage wrought on your carefully cultivated floral charges can unleash your primal side. I am not here to encourage 'manual crushing', but ... I understand.

Normally, I am the sort of soft-touch, lily-livered vegetarian who will spend £127 on surgery for a hamster, even though this is enough money to keep me in fresh hamsters till retirement, and it wasn't even a very friendly hamster anyway.

But provoked, I can turn. The gastropod genocides I have carried out in response to Dahlia devastation. Well, I'd rather not talk about it.

When you're done give your shoes a good wipe on the doormat and be sure to put your gloves in the wash.

Diseases

There are many different diseases that can affect plants, but as almost all chemical treatments have been banned, the exact strain need not concern you.

If you are gardening organically your choices are to either dig up the affected plants and take them to the council tip, or to live with the disfigurement. Anyone gardening within spore-travelling distance will thank you kindly to take the former option.

Disease usually occurs because the plant is not happy where it is. You might have pushed your luck too far, such as by planting a bog-dweller in full sun and free-draining soil even though I told you not to do this 48 pages ago.

It can also be because there is not enough air circulating around the plant, due to overcrowding (yes, I know I just told you to cram in the plants so as not to leave space for weeds: what can I say, it is a fine line).

If you decide to use chemical sprays note that they work as prevention not cure - this is not like trying to get rid of athlete's foot. Amputation is in order.

You will have to remove all dodgy-looking leaves, cut out all dodgy-looking shoots and stems and clear away any dodgy-looking leaves from the ground to stop fungal spores infecting the soil and thus anything that grows in it.

You will then have to wait for fresh new growth and then spray this to stop reinfection taking hold. Ideally you should also address the underlining problem, which might mean trying to give the plant more space, more light, giving it some manure or putting down bark to stop it drying out so easily. Or the opposite of all these things. Or just buy a new plant that is better suited to the conditions. From a good plant seller.

Never spray anything that is in flower. You might as well just chuck poison straight in the bees' faces. You monster.

The lawn

The well-manicured lawn is a monoculture, devoid of biodiversity. Whereas your lawn, with its buttercups, daisies, dandelions and clover, is excellent for nature.

Remind yourself of this often.

Now get out there (once it stops raining)

Gardening might never be any more than another household chore to you but I hope this book has armed you with enough knowledge to create something nicer to look out on to than death, disappointment and the physical manifestation of your own personal failure.

And just maybe, sometime in the future, you will find yourself looking at a pile of well-rotted horse manure with the same covetous eyes women in adverts have when they are looking at sparkly red shoes, and know you are smitten.

That is when you can buy one of those massive gardening books.

Printed in Poland
by Amazon Fulfillment
Poland Sp. z o.o., Wrocław